SUCCESS

UNDERSTANDING INADEQUACY AND HOW TO OVERCOME THOSE FEELINGS OF INADEQUACY

By Patricia A Carlisle

Introduction

I want to thank you and congratulate you for choosing the book, *"SUCCESS: UNDERSTANDING INADEQUACY, AND HOW TO OVERCOME THOSE FEELINGS OF INADEQUACY"*.

There are some people who feel inadequacy that feel good about themselves, build better personal relationships, and are more successful at work. They are confident when interacting with others, whether speaking in front of a group, over the telephone, or at a job interview.

Adequacy is a reflection of your self-esteem, and when you lack adequacy, you shy away from interacting with people. At work as well as in your personal life, low self-confidence impedes progress, and denies you many opportunities. Adequacy is a necessary skill in any interview situation, including making a presentation at an Assessment Center. In interviews, your level of adequacy will be obvious to interviewers, and could influence how they perceive you, and how they assess your credibility.

Knowing how to cope with feelings of inadequacy is very important for our well being. When we feel as if we are not good enough, we need to know how to bounce back. We need to understand how to overcome and continue on life's journey rather than being stuck in sorrow. This book will show you how to do just that.

Thanks again for choosing this book, I hope you enjoy it!

Patricia A. Carlisle, MSW, CBT

Patricia Carlisle- A Master Social Worker and a Cognitive Behavioral Therapist (CBT) gives out an expression of how important it is for an individual to take into consideration the concept of self-assessment to know what human, technical and conceptual skills they posses to perform or to achieve what they desire, or to deal with everyday life. However, every particular group of people has their own unique set of ideas, traditions and events including the frame of mind according to which people perform but there are many who faces problems and fail to maintain a healthy mind set affecting their behaviors and performance to those around them.

People like Patricia Carlisle are among those who have felt this urge of serving people and helping them out of their mental crisis towards a healthy life. She has experienced some close encounters in her personal life regarding mental health issues in her family and friends that has encouraged her to pursue this as her career.

Currently Patricia Carlisle is serving as a Certified On-Line Cognitive Behavioral Therapist with an extensive 15years of experience using Cognitive-Behavior Therapy Techniques. She envisions a world where everyone gets mental health treatment with no mental health stigma and to make it real she has already set up her own Holistic Measure Online Comprehensive Behavioral Healthcare Company after retiring from The Nord Center in The Partial Hospitalization Program (PHP) Dept for 5 years and Murtis H. Taylor Mental Health Center as a mental health counselor, psychological support technician and case manager for 10 years to emulsify her skills more professionally. Along with this, she has wrote down her passion as a clinician in 25 or more short books to help individuals and families get their life back, freeing them of the restraints of negative thinking, anxiety and depression by using different approaches. She is highly appreciated among her clients for her flexibility and professionalism of dealing with them graciously.

To reach her, make use of her direct website address: http://therapist2013.wix.com/e-therapy . As she is ready to inspire hope and contribute to health and well-being by providing the best online health care through comprehensive practice, education and research.

TABLE OF CONTENT

Chapter 1

WAYS TO COMBAT INADEQUACY

Let's take a look at some ways to deal with feelings of inadequacy. A good way to combat inadequacy is to think about all of the things you can do. Then think about the things that you can do well, or better than others. You should always be able to remind yourself of how special you are to the world.

Therefore, keep a journal or album of accomplishments, and awards you have achieved. This will be a good reference for you whenever you need to remind yourself of what you are capable of.

Next, after you bring to mind all of the things you can do, think of how, what you do well can prosper you. Why not allow one of your talents to bring you into a fortune, or at least make you a living? How fun would it be to do something you enjoy while getting paid for it? Try to find a way to put your skill or talent to use where it can be a blessing to you and others at the same time. This will be a constant reminder to you of how special you are to society because of your ability.

Encouraging others is another great way to cope with feelings of inadequacy. When you are encouraging others, you are not thinking about yourself. Instead, you are focused on pushing others toward their dreams, and making them feel great while doing so. In turn, the inspiration you give to other will come back to you.

An excellent way to defeat feeling inadequate is to not spend a lot of time alone. Instead, spend time with people so that you always have someone else to think about other than yourself. Some great ways to keep from being alone are to live with someone, volunteer regularly for a charity, or join a sports league. Having continuous company will keep you thought of, and keeps you in the presence of someone to reach out to.

A great way to stay away from thinking negatively about yourself is to stay away from negative environments. Do not spend your time in a place, or environment where bad things take place. Instead, spend your time in places where you can grow, and be encouraged as great things take place.

As you can see, there are multiple ways to overcome with feelings of inadequacy. Therefore, know that you are special, and let nobody, including yourself tell you any differently.

Chapter 2

UNDERSTANDING INADEQUACY
INADEQUACY FEELINGS

I am not good enough for this job.

I know I don't deserve it.

I don't know why I feel everyone is better than me.

I GUESS I AM INADEQUATE

If those phrases sound familiar then you probably have already experienced feelings of inadequacy.

People who feel inadequate think that they are less worthy than others. The bad thing about inadequacy is that it completely destroys self-confidence.

WHY DO SOME PEOPLE FEEL INADEQUATE?

Feeling inadequate could be the result of either considering others to be better than you or underestimating your own skills and abilities. People usually sell themselves short as a result of lack of self-confidence. Because they don't know whether they are valuable or not, they give everyone else the right to judge them. and then consider this judgment to be their unchangeable reality.

This may seem like a logical approach. but the problem here lies within the definition of the word JUDGMENT. Those people don't depend on verbal judgment, but rather misinterpret the events around them just to prove that they are inadequate. These events could be anything such as someone whispering behind them, or someone gazing at them in a way that they can't explain.

We all felt inadequate, not good enough at one point or another in our life, and tried to compensate for it somehow. Feelings of inadequacy have different roots, and can be connected to anything from being neglected as a child, workplace harassment, also known as bullying. We tell ourselves stories about how bad we are, or how we are going to fail anyway and we start believing them. Society, culture, and the power of the media contribute negatively to our feelings of inadequacy. They paint a perfect picture about success, beauty, money, fame and power that is totally unattainable. When we compare ourselves to this image of perfection, we are bound to believe we are a failure, and feel inadequate.

People may attempt to mask, or hide their feelings of inadequacy from themselves, and from others in a number of ways. Some people may isolate themselves socially, or otherwise close themselves off to the advances of others for fear of being truly "seen." Others may develop compulsions, such as over-spending or overeating, as a way to cope with feelings of inadequacy. And some people project their feelings of incompetence onto others as a way to avoid difficult emotions, or they may attempt to control others, or their environment in order to regain a sense of control when inadequacy leaves them feeling powerless.

PEOPLE WHO FEEL INADEQUATE MAY ALSO EXPERIENCE:

Anxiety, particularly with regards to performance.

Heightened sensitivity and self-criticism.

Reluctance to accept or trust in the affection of others.

Perception of failure.

Fear of rejection.

The inability to accept praise.

Feelings of powerlessness.

The inclination to conform or succumb to peer-pressure.

Chapter 3

INADEQUACY AND INFERIORITY

I can find almost no difference between the words inadequacy and inferiority. People who are inferior feel inadequate, and people who are inadequate feel inferior.

The key to getting rid of inadequacy is building self confidence, and getting rid of the inferiority complex if present. Does any of the above sound or feel familiar? If it does, this doesn't mean you need to see a therapist unless you suffer from acute anxiety or chronic depression, but it does mean you need help in understanding where all of this is coming from, what triggers you, and what are some of your typical coping behaviors.

A change in perspective and outlook can help you achieve more self-confidence, and increase your level of self-worth. A coach can help you do that by facilitating a self-discovery process in which you uncover your key values, strengths, and talents, and learn how to focus on them in other to get the most out of every situation and reach your highest potential. As long as you allow yourself to fall into the trap of shame, blame, and feelings of inadequacy, you are not in control.

Chapter 4

3 TRUTH TO REMEMBER WHEN YOU'RE FEELING INADEQUACY

So how do you battle these lies of inadequacy, and begin to understand the truth that you are valuable. Here are 3 truths to remember when you're feeling inadequacy.

1. YOU ARE VALUABLE FOR WHO YOU ARE, NOT FOR WHAT YOU DO.

You were created exclusively by God and for God. And because of that, you are valuable. There were no flaws in your design, and no errors in your construction. You are hand-made, custom-designed, and fully loaded by God; and because of that, you have immeasurable worth.

2. YOU HAVE GIFTS, EMBRACE THEM

Every person has gifts or strengths. If you don't know yours, I'd encourage you to ask five family members and friends this question, "In one or two words, what do you

think is my single greatest strength?". They'll all probably
give you similar answers. Those answer identifying your
area of giftedness will help you understand the truth that
you are valuable and have a lot to offer your family and the
world.

3. YOU WEREN'T MEANT TO DO THIS ALONE

If you're constantly putting on a front that you have it all
together, other people will start to believe that you really
do have it all together. So, I challenge you to be honest
with trusted friends and family. Share your struggles with
them, and let them help carry your burdens and encourage
you. Because the truth is: you were never meant to do this
alone.

Chapter 5

TIPS FOR UNSTICKING THE INADEQUATE FEELING BUTTON

There are times when we encounter other who just "rub us the wrong way." Have there ever been times in your life when others would say, or do something that gets under your skin or as I like to say, "Pushes your button?" The kind of people that irritate you every time they speak, or certain actions that just leave you feeling like you want to scream, and pull your hair out?

Some things or people may not push your buttons that hard. Some just cause you to feel minor irritation, or give you that "roll-your-eyes feelings." Whatever the case, have you wondered why these actions or behaviors push those buttons? Better yet, do you know what those buttons are?

Recently, I've had my "inadequate" button pushed. Usually when that one gets pushed, it gets stuck, and it takes a long time to become "unstuck," and everything around me seems to reinforce that feeling. I have, however, learned a couple valuable lessons and reminders from my recent experience. I will share some with you:

I am good enough. I just need to remind myself of that daily.

At times, the "it's-not-me-"it's-you" attitude can be helpful.

I do not have to absorb other people's insecurities.

Weak people need to hit you behind the knees in order to gain strength for themselves.

When you do the best that you know you can, that is what matters.

SOME WAYS TO COPE WITH INADEQUACY FEELINGS:

ACKNOWLEDGE IT'S AN UNCOMFORTABLE FEELING: Be aware of your buttons! There are times when we just have to be honest with ourselves, and admit that the situations we are in, or the feelings we are experiencing, place us in a lousy spot. We can't deal with something until we have named it. Name that bad situation!

BE WILLING TO TALK TO SOMEONE ABAOUT IT: Not just anyone, but someone who is positive and at the same time, someone who you trust for good advice. Nothing sinks you further into the depths of emotional hell than talking to a "Debbie Downer", or that "Negative Nance." Some people never have anything positive or uplifting to say! On the other hand, we do not want to reach out to those who will take your situation and turn it into theirs. You know, the people who like to say "ugh, you think that's bad, let me tell you about what happened to me!" This is not the time to be ignored or minimized.

JOURNAL

There's nothing better than writing down our thoughts and feelings, and being able to reflect on them a couple of days later. It helps us observe our growth and find simple lessons. I will forever sail on the ship of journaling. It has personally rescued me from negative emotions, and allowed me a nonjudgmental space to just let my thoughts and emotions flow. I trust my journal because it is a true reflection of my feelings, and it provides me with the forum to vent.

THINK ABOUT WHY THE BUTOTN THAT WAS PUSHED MADE YOU SO UNCOMFORTABLE

I have learned that many times, the things that others do that irritate me are the things about myself that I am either working hard not to be, or I am struggling to change. Be mindful of your emotional reaction to others' behavior. I have discovered that it teaches you a lot about yourself as well.

SEE WHAT YOU CAN CHANGE TO MAKE YOURSELF EMOTIONALLY HEALTHIER

I love teaching my clients about being honest with themselves. It is important both for their relationships with others and with themselves. Honesty with self, I have realized, is a bit more challenging than being honest with others. We try to fool ourselves into believing that things are not as bad as they are, or add more to the situation than is necessary. Sometimes the best way to deal with our character defects is admitting that we can do something to assist the process of change, and that it does not have to be someone else's responsibility.

Chapter 6

STEPS TO OVERCOME THOSE FEELINGS OF INADEQUACY

Step 1: Recognize the problem: All people undergo brief periods of depression and inadequacy from time to time, but most people quickly move past this, and do not allow these periods to permanently define their self worth, or allow others to capitalize on it.   This leads many people with a serious problem to believe that their inadequacy is normal, and that most people have the same view of themselves.

The view that having low self esteem is perfectly natural and normal often means that people with a problem do not recognize it as such. If you sincerely lack self confidence, and believe yourself to be lesser than just a couple of months – there is probably something wrong.   The first step to combating the problem of inadequacy is recognizing the problem as such, and deciding to put forth a conscious effort to correct it.

Step 2: Recognizing no one is perfect: Building upon the first step, you have to recognize that no one is perfect, and that we all have failings. However, this reality does not prevent most people from aggressively pursuing their lives, and building up the confidence they need to accomplish their goals, and successfully operate in society. The same holds true for you: no, you are not perfect, but this lack of perfection should not be a stumbling block to you achieving what you need and want in life.

Further, this lack of perfection makes you no worse than anyone else, and has nothing to do with your inherent worth as a human being. Everyone is stumbling along through life making mistakes, correcting them, and moving on, and you should be doing this as well.

So, the second step to becoming more confident is to recognize that you are like everyone else, imperfect, but quite capable of surviving despite of this.

Step 3 Focus on your strengths: Though people suffering from inadequacy may not realize it, everyone is good at some things, and bad at others. Focus on your personal strengths, the things you are good at, and do not dwell on those things you are not good at. Recognizing your strengths, and using them to the best of your ability allows you to build up your confidence, as well as your self esteem.

Even if you are not particularly impressed by your own talents, work with what you have, and build these talents as much as you can. Further, once you recognize your talents you can find others that also enjoy these things, and practice with them. Playing to your strengths and recognizing – though not dwelling on – your weaknesses will allow to build up your confidence, and improve how you view yourself.

This means the third step is to recognize your strengths and weaknesses for what they are, and focus on building up your strengths, and not dwelling on your weaknesses.

Step 4 Recognize and accept differences: Like it or not, no two people are exactly the same. Some people will always be better than you at some things just as you will always be better than some people at other things. This is just how the world is, so judging yourself, and your self worth by the standards set by someone else is a mistake. In life you may have to compete with others on a regular basis, but do not define yourself, or base your worth on the outcome of these contests.

More often than not, there will always be someone out there that is better at this than you are, but this does not make you any less of a person. Just accept the notion that you cannot be the very best at everything, and do not judge yourself too harshly for failing to live up to the standard set by someone else. By all means do your best, but do not let failure define you.

The fourth and final step to feeling better about yourself is to accept that someone out there is probably better than you at any given thing, so accept doing the best that you can.

Chapter 7

HOW TO OVERCOME FEELINGS OF INADEQUACY

SPEND TIME IN THE SCRIPTURES: Even if it's reading the same verse(s) over again and again! Some of my favorites are:

"Thou wilt keep him in perfect peach whose mind is stay on Thee.." (Isaiah 26:3)

"Being confident of this very thing, that He which hath begun a good work in you will perform it (or complete it)..." (Philippians 1:6)

"for I know the plans I have for you," declares the LORD, "plans to prosper you and not to harm you, plans to give you hope and a future." (Jeremiah 29:11)

REMEMBER THAT EVERY DAY IS A CHOICE: We can choose to believe that worst about ourselves, or we can choose to believe that we are good enough and that there's nothing that can come to us that isn't good for us. If we choose to be miserable and unhappy, we can find a lot of good reasons to keep being miserable and unhappy. However, if we choose to have peace, we can find a lot of reasons to have peace. It works both ways. We have to make the choice to believe that we are good enough. (Trust me, it isn't always easy, but it does pay off!)

WRITE DOWN YOUR FEELINGS AND TAKE OUT THE TRASH: Writing down my feelings has become a game changer for me. When I take the time to sit down and write out my feelings, I get a clearer picture of the "why" behind those feelings. Sometimes it is because I haven't taken the time for myself that I need to take; like reading a book, taking a long bath, or playing the piano. Sometimes it's because I haven't taken the time that I need with my Heavenly Father. Other times it may be the time of the month, or I may not have been eating right. There are lots of triggers, and when you take the time to start investigating, you'll find those things.

After writing down my feelings, and finding the things that triggered my emotional hang ups, I take time to clean up those emotions. Sometimes I go outside and read out loud the things I wrote down. Other times I sit on the couch and read them quietly, and pray for God to give me wisdom in learning how to deal with them. I NEVER read them to another person. This list is only between me and God. Once I've read through the words and the emotions, I find a way to get rid of them (take out the trash). One of the most effective ways is to burn them, seriously. You should try it and experience the release for yourself.

REMEMBER THAT WE ARE NOT DEFINED BY OUR FEELINGS: Just because we feel a certain way doesn't mean we are that way. We need to understand that feelings do not define who we are. When we are experiencing an uncomfortable emotion, we should know that it has not downgraded our character, or the heart of who we are. It just means that for a moment, a very small second of time, we feel a certain way about ourselves.

We need to extend the same grace and mercy to ourselves as we would our friends. When we treat ourselves as humans instead of emotional feelings, we extend the ability to reframe those self-limiting thoughts and beliefs, and keep them from defining who we are.

YOU ARE ALWAYS GOOD ENOUGH TO TRY, AND THAT'S WHAT COUNTS! If you never try, you'll never achieve. Give yourself a chance and see what happens. Ten years from now, you'll be more disappointed by the things you didn't do more than the things you did.

THERE IS ALWAYS SOMETHING SMALL THAT YOU CAN DO: Sometimes taking a small step has more meaning than a huge step. If you want to go upstairs, you can't just stand at the bottom and wish your way up. One small step may end up being the biggest step you'll take in your life. There is nothing stopping you from moving forward one tiny step at a time.

YOUR DON'T NEED EVERYONE ELSE'S APPROVAL: For me, this is one of the hardest lessons I've learned. Well, I'm still learning it...daily. Stop listening to what the world says you should want/be/do. Start listening to YOU. Be who you are meant to be. There are only a few people in your life who will be completely true to you, YOU should be one of them! If you have a dream, go for it. Don't let anyone keep you from being who you are meant to be, and doing what you are meant to do.

YOU HAVE TO WORK HARD: There is a reason that the words self-love, self-respect, and self-acceptance have the word "self" in them. YOU have to respect yourself, love yourself, and accept you. That's hard to do at times, but we can't receive them from anyone else. It's hard for others to give you the respect you deserve until you can respect yourself. It is the same with love, acceptance, and all the other things in life. Believe me, it's hard work, but so worth it!

YOU HAVE MADE THE BEST OF WHAT LIFE HAVE HANDED YOU: So life has handed you a basket of lemons. Yep, I hear it all the time too – "When life hands you lemons, make lemonade!" It gets old, but the truth is it's got a lot of meaning. Life is full of disappointments. Life isn't fair. Should we sit and feel sorry for ourselves because we don't have it as good as someone else? No. We make the best of what we are given. We go on smiling. Smiling doesn't mean that we have no troubles, or that we're happy with everything. Smiling means that we are strong, and that we are smart enough to accept what comes, and make the best of it. Smiling can change our life!

YOU ARE TRYING: Never give up! Never quit trying. If you never quit trying, you'll be stronger, more patient, and a winner. It's not the one who is the strongest who wins the most. It's the people who keep on trying no matter what. I think we would all be surprised to know how many people that we have the utmost respect for have had times of not feeling good enough. The people we think the most of have known despair, heart break, and misery. But they didn't give up because they felt inadequate. They have given us even more to look forward to because they have learned the art of getting up when they were down, loving and living instead of losing, and they are a source of wisdom and understanding from their own hurts and failures.

- o Step out of your comfort zone, and attempt new tasks. Create novel strategies for action, meet new people and visit new places.

- o Develop your knowledge and stay current. Keeping informed will give you confidence. Extend the breadth of your information gathering so you are current, and share up-to-date rather than outdated information.

- o Recognize and value the importance of continuing to learn-lifelong learning. It does not have to be a formal course, as we learn in different ways, and from various experiences-our own, those of our families and friends, and sometimes, even from strangers.

- o Develop strong thinking skills. Being a Mom and responding to numerous questions from your child has prepared you for this, so show how much you have learned. You will have more successful outcomes when you are able to think quickly when on your feel-or seat-in an interview and respond well to questions asked by interviewers.

- o When you cannot find a suitable response, ask for time to address it later, before the end of the interview. This shows you are thinking, and prepared to do your best.

- o Don't let setbacks get you down. Identify what you have learned from each situation, and ensure you don't repeat the actions that caused them.

- Learn to express your ideas-fluently, and in a way that engages people. Hone your skills by signing up to a public speaking, or presentation skills course, or get advice from a Trainer or Speaker who appears confident and demonstrates the skills of speech craft.

- Model the behavior of confident people you encounter, especially those people with whom you interact regularly.

- Visualize yourself in situations where you were comfortable and felt confident. Now remember how you felt, and retain that feeling of pleasure for a few seconds. If you can recreate that feeling you'll find that you can actually change the way you feel right now. This technique is known as 'anchoring'. Use this anchoring technique when you feel the need to boost your self-confidence.

- Recognize your own abilities and experience, do not undervalue them. If you can mentally 'pat yourself on the back' about what you know already, your self-esteem and confidence will increase. Give yourself that much-needed and well-deserved boost!

- If your inferiority stems from the company you keep, stop associating with all those who make you feel small, inadequate, or insecure of your place and position.

- If the causes of your feeling of inferiority are your tasks at work or at social functions, stop accepting them. Know your limitations, and the extent of your abilities. Refuse to become involved in anything that you cannot follow through successfully just because it puts you in the limelight for a while.

- If people with names or titles make you feel small, self-conscious and insignificant, avoid close contact with them. Why play "second fiddle" to them? Associate with those who come nearer to your standards, and those who make you feel comfortable.

- Place a price on yourself, on your knowledge, ability, dignity and self-respect. Refuse to service as a mat for others to walk upon. Speak up. Voice your displeasure, your likes or dislikes. Do it again and again, and before long your fear of speaking up and your feeling of inferiority will be gone.

- It is commendable to seek higher levels but only when you have prepared yourself, and not at the expense of your self-esteem and self-confidence.

- If you want to get rid of your feeling of inferiority stay within your bounds, and do not overreach yourself. Find out what you do best, work diligently at it until you excel at it, and then capitalize upon it.

- Sell yourself on the fact that you are as good, as capable, as important, and even better in some respects, as those with whom you usually associate.

- If your inferiority stems from oversensitivity, or self-consciousness it may be due to the fact that you thank yourself too seriously. Do not assume that people have you on their minds and talk constantly about you. This is not the case. Rid yourself of these thoughts and your self-consciousness will gradually disappear.

- If you feel you are not like, or wanted, or welcomed when you come in company with certain people, it may be due to the fact that you expect too much. Perhaps you wear your heart on your sleeve, and feel hurt when people fail to notice it.

o If you intensely dislike what you are doing, but keep at it halfheartedly because you are afraid to make a change you are doing an injustice to others, and are unfair to yourself. Make the necessary changes.

o If you have been too willing to take "second best" if you are forever apologizing for living or for taking up room, how can you expect others to value you as a person? You have definite capabilities which you and you alone can develop and capitalize upon.

o Remind yourself that you are not who other people think or say you are.

o Remind yourself that everybody makes mistakes at times has areas of weakness, and things they want to change.

o Remind yourself of ways in which you've grown and changed with time. You're not who you once were – so celebrate how far you've come.

o Also, the ending isn't written and the future isn't fixed. You're free to change your image, and an old identity.

o Identify the lies you have believed about yourself and work on changing them so they're more accurate and true. Also, don't reinforce those lies by acting like you think they're true.

o Remember that your feelings are not the same as facts. Don't live based on your feelings..as that will keep you trapped.

o Hang out with those who see, and who appreciate, your worth. And take their words to heart, and let them help to build you up.

Chapter 8

OVERCOMING FEELINGS OF INADEQUACY WITH CLINICAL HYPNOSIS

In the course of a lifetime, everyone has moments where they feel a lack of self-confidence, or feel inadequate in some way. This is part of the human experience, and these feelings often pass. But if you have pervasive feelings of inadequacy most of the time, your sense of inadequacy can be a major stumbling block in your life.

FEELINGS OF INADEQUACY CAN BE LONGSTANDING, OR THEY CAN SEEM TO COME FROM "NOWHER"

For many people, feelings of being inadequate, such as feeling "I'm not good enough", or "I'm not lovable, "have been part of their awareness for a s long as they can remember. Other people often experience these feelings as having come seemingly, from "nowhere." For these people, the experience of feeling inadequate, when they normally feel confident, can be very confusing, and they often wonder, "Why is this happening to me?"

DISCOVERING WHAT TRIGGERED FEELINGS OF INADEQUACY

Often, when feelings of being inadequate seem to come from "nowhere," there is a precipitating event that triggered this feeling, but the person experiencing this might not know what it is. Working with a skilled hypnotherapist can help clients to discover the triggering event so that clients can overcome feelings of low self worth.

In most cases, the hypnotherapist will work with clients to help them discover, if possible, the first event that triggered this feeling. The first event might be a long forgotten memory of when the client was a child that gets triggered during a current event. This can be tricky because memory isn't always reliable.

EARLIER MEMORIES CAN LAY "DORMAT" FOR A LONG TIME BEFORE THEY'RE TRIGGERED

It's not unusual, for earlier memories of shame and humiliation to lay "dormant" for a long time—only to get triggered by a similar recent event. It can be one traumatic memory, or it can be a series of traumatic memories that get triggered. It's often hard to know why a particular recent event triggers these feelings, and other similar events might not. But the most people usually has a gut feeling, while in a relaxed hypnotic state, of the connection between the old memories and the recent event.

GETTING HELP

Whether your experience with low self confidence is a recent development, or a longstanding problem, working with a skilled hypnotherapist can help you to overcome this problem. As I've mentioned in earlier articles, hypnotherapy isn't always quick, or a magic bullet cure, but it's often very effective in helping clients overcome emotional problems.

Chapter 9

DON'T PROJECT YOUR FEELINGS OF INADEQUACY ONTO OTHERS

Self-loathing people (those who experience intense feelings of inadequacy) are characterized by intensely negative thinking about themselves, in particular their talents and abilities, their self-worth, and their ability to be loved. (As you may know, this is also commonly associated with depression, from which I am sure many such people suffer). I've written here before about how hard it can be for someone who loves a self-loathing person to cope with this. Another thing that puts stress on such relationships is the self-loathing person's projection of the negative attitudes he or she feels towards themselves onto what other people say to them.

It is a fact of language that it's vague any statement can be interpreted an infinite number of ways, even when intonation and tone are taken into account. A seemingly innocuous statement like "isn't the sky blue today" can be taken a number of different ways depending on how a person chooses to hear it. It could be an expression of joy, a statement of appreciation for the beauty of nature, or a snide comment on the mood of the person to whom it is said. OK, maybe that last one was a bit extreme, but likely not unfamiliar. A person who persistently thinks negatively about himself or herself may also assume that others think the same way, no matter how strenuously they deny it. So if a self-loathing person regards himself as gloomy, he may project that onto others assuming they find him ungrateful and voila.

Likewise, if the self-loathing person thinks of themselves as stupid, and someone ribs them about a minor slip-up he or she made that day, they may take that as serious criticism rather than an innocent joke. Of course, the other person didn't mean it that way, but the self-loathing person hears it that way nonetheless, because that's how they think of them self, so that's how they assume others (really) see them too.

With respect to relationships, many self-loathing people feel unworthy of their significant others affection. So, any criticism, no matter how slight or humorously intended may be take to the extreme, and lead the self-loathing person to thin, "OK, so now we're in agreement I suck." Does this mean, if you're in a relationship with a self-loathing person, you can never criticize him or her, and instead you must provide constant coddling and positive reinforcement? Of course not no one should be immune from criticism, even if they're naturally disposed to take it harder than intended.

One problem that self-loathing people often have is that they place too much emphasis on negative reinforcement (criticism), and too little positive reinforcement (praise).

Praise is assumed to be insincere or underserved, while criticism is assumed to be understated and very deserved, confirming the person's own beliefs about themselves. So lavish as much praise of them as you can, but they'll still only remember when you told them they put too much sugar in your coffee, which in their mind confirms that you think just as little of them as they do.

For the partners of self-loathing people, I would simply advise not that praise be given more often, but that you make sure the other person listen to it, really hears it, and understands how sincere it is. By the same token, you don't have to criticize them less often, but perhaps make an effort to ensure that it is taken only in the spirit intended—too much sugar is fast, too much sugar, not a death sentence for the relationship.

To the self-loathing person, I would say that regardless of how you feel about yourself, you should give other people the benefit of the doubt that they are sincere when they praise you. But the same token, when others criticize you, try to hear just what they say, no more. It is all too easy to read too much into what people say, especially when you impute your own feelings of inadequacy onto their words. But that is your problem, not theirs particularly when the other person only wants to love you.

Conclusion

Thank you again for choosing this book!

We all struggle with feelings of inadequacy at one point or another in life. Instead of staying trapped in the mindset of thinking you have nothing to offer, remind yourself of these important truths.

Challenge yourself always to find the positive in negative situations. Most important, I will try to remember that it is okay to have a bad day, because it makes the good days even better.

If there are things you always wanted to do but somehow never got around to them. Get started on them now! Work at them now! It may not be easy, but go on just the same.

By trying over and over again, your sense of inadequacy will vanish, and your feeling of inferiority will disappear

Finally, if you enjoyed this book, would you be kind enough to leave a review for this book on Amazon? It'd be greatly appreciated!

Thank you and good luck!

Preview Of 'INSECURITY: STOP THE INSECURITY AND LEARN HOW TO OVERCOME JEALOUSY AND BUILD SELF ESTEEM'

Chapter 1

HOW TO STOP INSECURITY

Insecurity is not bad: People feel bad when they feel insecure because it's commonly believed that insecurity is a bad emotion that has no useful role in improving ones live.

However when taking a closer look at the cause of insecurity you will find that insecurity is just a message sent by your brain trying to tell you one of the following things:

- I am not sure of my ability to do this task.

- I think I might be moving in the wrong direction or...

- I might lose what I already have.

Insecurity is one of the strongest motivational forces

We human beings are either motivation by rewards or plain avoidance. Those who understand the fact that insecurity is just a message manage to completely eliminate their insecurities by providing reassurance to their minds. For example if you felt insecure about your job then improving your skills, taking additional courses, working harder and improving your CV will surely eliminate your insecurity.

It's as if insecurity is the key driving force that pushes people to new achievements that they wouldn't have achieved otherwise if they didn't feel insecure.

But sadly not all people manage to take advantage of the insecurity feelings, some people fail to understand the nature of the insecurity feelings and so live with them for extended periods of time or use quick fixes every now and then to temporary regulate their mood. Quick fixes can range from food, smoking, relationships up to drugs and self harm. The ultimate destination for people who use quick fixes is depression!! If you kept using quick fixes then suddenly you will find yourself facing a major depression as a result of the accumulated problems.

PATRICIA A. CARLISLE

INSECURE

Stop the Insecurity and Learn
how to Overcome Jealousy
and Build Self-Esteem

Check out the rest of (INSECURE: Stop the Insecurity and Learn how to Overcome Jealousy and Build Self-Esteem) on Amazon.com

Check Out My Other Books

Below you'll find some of my other popular books that are popular on Amazon and Kindle as well. Alternatively, you can visit my author page on Amazon to see other work done by me.

LETTING GO: LEARN HOW TO EMBRACE THE FUTURE.

A GUIDANCE TO MENTAL TRAINING: LEARN HOW TO DEVELOP MENTAL RESILIENCE.

MINDSET: HOW YOU CAN BECOME POWERFUL AND ACHIEVE SUCCESS ON YOUR TERMS.

BOUNDARIES IN RELATIONSHIPS: How to Develop boundaries in MARRIAGE and DATING.

COMMUNICATION SKILLS AND TECHNIQUES FOR DUMMIES.

ASSERTIVENESS: HOW TO STAND UP FOR YOURSELF AND BE STRONG IN EVERY SITUATION.

FAILURE IS NOT AN OPTION: Learn How to Overcome The Fear Of Failing.

MINDULNESS EXERCISES FOR BEGINNERS.

BONUS: SUBSCRIBE TO THE FREE BOOK

Beginners Guide to Yoga & Meditation

"Stressed out? Do You Feel Like The World Is Crashing Down Around You? Want To Take A Vacation That Will Relax Your Mind, Body And Spirit? Well this Easy To Read Step By Step

E-Book Makes It All Possible!"

Instructions on how to join our mailing list, and receive a free copy of "Yoga and Meditation" can be found in any of my Kindle eBooks.

NOTES

NOTES

www.ingramcontent.com/pod-product-compliance
Lightning Source LLC
Chambersburg PA
CBHW070412190526
45169CB00003B/1225